MEDIEVAL CATS

Coloring Book
for
Cat Lovers

A Great Cat Production

by

L.A. Vocelle

ISBN: 0692660402
ISBN: 978-0692660409

www.thegreatcat.org

DEDICATION

This book is dedicated to my little love, Beseechy Runtus. We will meet again.

Medieval Cat Grooming Itself
Morgan Library, 15th Century

Cats Chasing Mice, Bodleian Library, 1511

Cat with Zither
Belgian Book of Hours, 1470
Morgan Library, New York

Horaedad Usum Rothomagensem Manuscript
1401-1500
National Library of France

Three Cats and a Rat
Harleian Bestiary, 13th Century
British Museum

Cat Crouching on a Mound of Earth
English Bestiary, 14th Century
University of Cambridge

Cat Playing a Psaltery
Belgian Book of Hours, 1470
Morgan Library

Cat and Mouse
Book of Hours, 14-15th Century
Morgan Library

Cat and Fiddle
French Book of Hours, 1470
Morgan Library

Cats and Rats
Workshop Bestiary, England, 1185
Morgan Library

Lion
Persian Bestiary, 12-13th Century
University of St. Andrews

Bodeian Bestiary
Bodeian Library, England

**Cat Playing with Ball of Cotton, Tapisserie de la Vie Seigneuriale, 1520
Musée de Cluny**

Cat Jumping from a Well, Unknown Manuscript, 14-15th Century

Cat Playing the Bagpipes, Book of Hours, Paris, 1460, Morgan Library

Cats, The Book of Wonders of the Age, Persian, 12-13th Century, University of St. Andrews

Three Attitudes of the Lion, 1511, Bodeleian Library

White Cat, Book of Hours, 1500, Bibliothèque de l'Arsenal, Paris

Cat and Mouse, French Book of Hours, 1500-1515, Morgan Library

Cat, Le Livre de la chasse, Gaston Phoebus, 1407, Paris, Morgan Library

43